BIRD VIEWING AREAS

1. West Nose Creek Park/Confluence Park
2. Nose Hill Park
3. Bowmont Park
4. University of Calgary Campus
5. Bowness Park
6. Edworthy Park
7. Strathcona Park
8. Bow Valley Provincial Park
9. Sibbald Creek Trail
10. Griffith Woods Park
11. Weaselhead Natural Environment Area
12. Bridlewood Creek Wetlands
13. Sheep River Provincial Park
14. Fish Creek Provincial Park
15. Wyndham-Carseland Provincial Park
16. Carburn Park
17. Beaverdam Flats
18. Inglewood Bird Sanctuary
19. Saint Patrick's Island
20. Sadler's Slough

Waterford Press produces reference guides that introduce novices to nature, science, survival and outdoor recreation. Product information is featured on the website: www.waterfordpress.com

ISBN 978-1-58355-548-4 $7.95 U.S.

50795

9 781583 555484

8 84682 00935

T0123936

10 9 8 7 6 5 4 3 2 1   Made in the USA

A POCKET NATURALIST® GUIDE

CALGARY BIRDS

A Folding Pocket Guide to Familiar Species

CALGARY BIRDS – A Folding Pocket Guide to Familiar Species

Kavanagh/Leung

WATERBIRDS & NEARSHORE BIRDS

Common Loon
Gavia immer To 3 ft. (90 cm)

Winter
Summer

Tundra Swan
Cygnus columbianus
To 4.5 ft. (1.4 m)
Note yellow mark on black bill.

Eared Grebe
Podiceps nigricollis
To 14 in. (35 cm)
Note black neck and golden ear tufts.

Western Grebe
Aechmophorus occidentalis
To 25 in. (63 cm)

Canada Goose
Branta canadensis
To 45 in. (1.14 m)

Green-winged Teal
Anas crecca To 15 in. (38 cm)

Red-necked Grebe
Podiceps grisegena To 19 in. (48 cm)

Blue-winged Teal
Spatula discors To 16 in. (40 cm) ♂

Northern Shoveler
Spatula clypeata To 20 in. (50 cm)
Named for its large spatulate bill. ♂

Mallard
Anas platyrhynchos To 28 in. (70 cm) ♂

Canvasback ♂
Aythya valisineria To 2 ft. (60 cm)
Note sloping forehead and black bill.

Redhead
Aythya americana To 22 in. (55 cm) ♂

Bufflehead
Bucephala albeola To 15 in. (38 cm) ♀

WATERBIRDS & NEARSHORE BIRDS

Ruddy Duck
Oxyura jamaicensis To 16 in. (40 cm)
Note cocked tail.

Common Merganser ♂
Mergus merganser To 27 in. (68 cm)
Note slender profile and thin red bill.

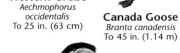

Lesser Scaup
Aythya affinis To 18 in. (45 cm)
Note peaked crown.

American Wigeon
Mareca americana To 23 in. (58 cm)

Northern Pintail
Anas acuta To 30 in. (75 cm)

Common Goldeneye ♂
Bucephala clangula To 18 in. (45 cm)

Gadwall
Mareca strepera To 21 in. (53 cm)

American Coot
Fulica americana To 16 in. (40 cm)

Spotted Sandpiper
Actitis macularius
To 8 in. (20 cm)
Breast is spotted.

Double-crested Cormorant
Phalacrocorax auritus
To 3 ft. (90 cm)
Note orange-yellow throat patch.

Wilson's Snipe
Gallinago delicata
To 12 in. (30 cm)

Lesser Yellowlegs
Tringa flavipes
To 10 in. (25 cm)

Wilson's Phalarope
Phalaropus tricolor
To 9 in. (23 cm)

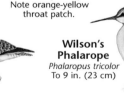

WATERBIRDS & NEARSHORE BIRDS

Marbled Godwit
Limosa fedoa
To 20 in. (50 cm)
Long bill is slightly upturned.

Long-billed Dowitcher
Limnodromus scolopaceus
To 12 in. (30 cm)
Breeding male has a rusty breast.

Killdeer
Charadrius vociferus
To 12 in. (30 cm)
Note two breast bands.

American Avocet
Recurvirostra americana
To 20 in. (50 cm)

American White Pelican
Pelecanus erythrorhynchos
To 5 ft. (1.5 m)

Black-crowned Night-Heron
Nycticorax nycticorax
To 28 in. (70 cm)

Great Blue Heron
Ardea herodias
To 4.5 ft. (1.4 m)

Willet
Tringa semipalmata
To 17 in. (43 cm)
Wings flash black-and-white in flight.

Franklin's Gull
Leucophaeus pipixcan
To 14 in. (35 cm)

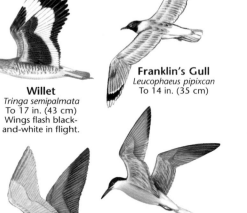

Black Tern
Chlidonias niger
To 10 in. (25 cm)
Head and belly are black.

Common Tern
Sterna hirundo
To 15 in. (38 cm)
Note black cap and forked tail. Orange bill is black-tipped.

Ring-billed Gull
Larus delawarensis
To 20 in. (50 cm)
Bill has dark ring.

California Gull
Larus californicus albertaensis
To 23 in. (58 cm)
Note black and red spots on its bill.

DOVES, WOODPECKERS, ETC.

Gray Partridge
Perdix perdix
To 14 in. (35 cm)
Has a 'U'-shaped belly patch.

Sharp-tailed Grouse
Tympanuchus phasianellus
To 20 in. (50 cm)
Tail is short and pointed.

Ruffed Grouse
Bonasa umbellus
To 19 in. (48 cm)
Note black tail band.

Rufous Hummingbird
Selasphorus rufus
To 3.5 in. (9 cm)

Ring-necked Pheasant
Phasianus colchicus
To 3 ft. (90 cm)

Ruby-throated Hummingbird
Archilochus colubris
To 3.5 in. (9 cm)

Rock Pigeon
Columba livia
To 13 in. (33 cm)

Mourning Dove
Zenaida macroura
To 13 in. (33 cm)
Call is a mournful--ooah-woo-woo-woo.

Northern Flicker
Colaptes auratus
To 13 in. (33 cm)
Wing and tail linings are red.

Downy Woodpecker
Dryobates pubescens
To 6 in. (15 cm)
The similar hairy woodpecker is larger and has a longer bill.

Hairy Woodpecker
Dryobates villosus
To 10 in. (25 cm)

Yellow-bellied Sapsucker
Sphyrapicus varius
To 9 in. (23 cm)
Drills holes in trees and feeds on the sap and insects that collect there.

Belted Kingfisher
Megaceryle alcyon
To 14 in. (35 cm)

Black Swift
Cypseloides niger
To 7 in. (18 cm)

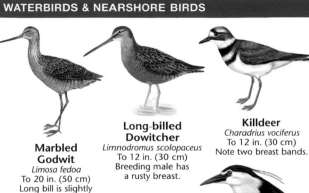

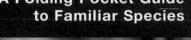

BIRDS OF PREY

Red-tailed Hawk
Buteo jamaicensis
To 25 in. (63 cm)
Note long, square-edged tail and striped breast.

Sharp-shinned Hawk
Accipiter striatus
To 14 in. (35 cm)

Swainson's Hawk
Buteo swainsoni
To 22 in. (55 cm)
Note dark terminal tail band. The dark morph of this species is dark brown below.

Osprey
Pandion haliaetus
To 2 ft. (60 cm)
Found near water, it feeds on fish.

Cooper's Hawk
Accipiter cooperii
To 20 in. (50 cm)
Note long, rounded white-tipped tail.

American Kestrel
Falco sparverius
To 12 in. (30 cm)

Merlin
Falco columbarius
To 14 in. (35 cm)
Tail is heavily banded.

Bald Eagle
Haliaeetus leucocephalus
To 40 in. (1 m)

Northern Harrier
Circus hudsonius
To 22 in. (55 cm)
Note V-shaped flight profile and white rump.

Rough-legged Hawk
Buteo lagopus
To 2 ft. (60 cm)
Note dark banded white tail and dark 'wrists'.

Short-eared Owl
Asio flammeus
To 17 in. (43 cm)
Call is a high, raspy barking.

Great Horned Owl
Bubo virginianus
To 25 in. (63 cm)
Call is a resonant – hoo-HOO-hoooo.

PERCHING BIRDS

Least Flycatcher
Empidonax minimus
To 5 in. (13 cm)

Western Wood-Pewee
Contopus sordidulus
To 7 in. (18 cm)
Note 2 narrow white wing bars.

Eastern Kingbird
Tyrannus tyrannus
To 8 in. (20 cm)
Note broad white tail band.

Olive-sided Flycatcher
Contopus cooperi
To 8 in. (20 cm)
Note white stripe down center of breast.

Bank Swallow
Riparia riparia
To 6 in. (15 cm)
Note breast band.

Cliff Swallow
Petrochelidon pyrrhonota
To 6 in. (15 cm)
Tail is square-edged.

Tree Swallow
Tachycineta bicolor
To 6 in. (15 cm)

Barn Swallow
Hirundo rustica
To 8 in. (20 cm)
Note deeply forked tail.

White-breasted Nuthatch
Sitta carolinensis
To 6 in. (15 cm)

Brown Creeper
Certhia americana
To 5 in. (13 cm)
Note downcurved bill. Forages for insects on tree trunks.

Red-breasted Nuthatch
Sitta canadensis
To 4.5 in. (11 cm)

Black-capped Chickadee
Poecile atricapillus
To 6 in. (15 cm)
Name-saying call is – chick-a-dee-dee-dee.

Mountain Chickadee
Poecile gambeli
To 6 in. (15 cm)

Boreal Chickadee
Poecile hudsonicus
To 6 in. (15 cm)

PERCHING BIRDS

Red-eyed Vireo
Vireo olivaceus
To 6 in. (15 cm)

Golden-crowned Kinglet
Regulus satrapa
To 3.5 in. (9 cm)

Marsh Wren
Cistothorus palustris
To 5 in. (13 cm)
Note white stripes on back and white eyebrow stripe.

House Wren
Troglodytes aedon
To 5 in. (13 cm)

Ruby-crowned Kinglet
Regulus calendula
To 4 in. (10 cm)

Mountain Bluebird
Sialia currucoides
To 7 in. (18 cm)

American Robin
Turdus migratorius
To 11 in. (28 cm)

Swainson's Thrush
Catharus ustulatus
To 7 in. (18 cm)

Varied Thrush
Ixoreus naevius
To 11 in. (28 cm)

Townsend's Solitaire
Myadestes townsendi
To 8 in. (20 cm)
Gray bird has a white eye ring and buffy wing patches.

Horned Lark
Eremophila alpestris
To 8 in. (20 cm)

Brown Thrasher
Toxostoma rufum
To 12 in. (30 cm)

Blue Jay
Cyanocitta cristata
To 14 in. (35 cm)

PERCHING BIRDS

Gray Catbird
Dumetella carolinensis
To 9 in. (23 cm)
Call is similar to a cat's meow.

Yellow-rumped Warbler
Setophaga coronata
To 6 in. (15 cm)
Note yellow rump, crown and throat.

MacGillivray's Warbler
Geothlypis tolmiei
To 6 in. (15 cm)
Note gray hood and broken eye ring.

Wilson's Warbler
Cardellina pusilla
To 5 in. (13 cm)
Note black crown.

Tennessee Warbler
Oreothlypis peregrina
To 5 in. (13 cm)
Plumage is greenish above and white below.

Yellow Warbler
Setophaga petechia
To 5 in. (13 cm)

Warbling Vireo
Vireo gilvus
To 5 in. (13 cm)
Note light breast and eye stripe.

Common Yellowthroat
Geothlypis trichas
To 5 in. (13 cm)

American Dipper
Cinclus mexicanus
To 9 in. (23 cm)
Aquatic songbird is found near clear-running streams.

Bohemian Waxwing
Bombycilla garrulus
To 8 in. (20 cm)
Red wing marks look like waxy droplets.

Cedar Waxwing
Bombycilla cedrorum
To 7 in. (18 cm)

Western Tanager
Piranga ludoviciana
To 7 in. (18 cm)

American Pipit
Anthus rubescens
To 7 in. (18 cm)
Frequently wags its white-edged tail while walking.

PERCHING BIRDS

Canada Jay
Perisoreus canadensis
To 14 in. (35 cm)

American Crow
Corvus brachyrhynchos
To 22 in. (55 cm)
Call is a distinct – caw.

Common Raven
Corvus corax
To 27 in. (68 cm)
Call is a hoarse croak.

Red-winged Blackbird
Agelaius phoeniceus
To 9 in. (23 cm)

Yellow-headed Blackbird
Xanthocephalus xanthocephalus
To 11 in. (28 cm)

European Starling
Sturnus vulgaris
To 8 in. (20 cm)

Brown-headed Cowbird
Molothrus ater
To 7 in. (18 cm)

Baltimore Oriole
Icterus galbula
To 8 in. (20 cm)

Black-billed Magpie
Pica hudsonia
To 22 in. (55 cm)

Northern Shrike
Lanius borealis
To 11 in. (28 cm)
Note hooked bill and black mask.

Brewer's Blackbird
Euphagus cyanocephalus
To 9 in. (23 cm)

Common Grackle
Quiscalus quiscula
To 14 in. (35 cm)

PERCHING BIRDS

Pine Siskin
Spinus pinus
To 5 in. (13 cm)

White-throated Sparrow
Zonotrichia albicollis
To 7 in. (18 cm)
Note white throat and yellow spot in front of eye.

House Sparrow
Passer domesticus
To 6 in. (15 cm)

Lark Sparrow
Chondestes grammacus
To 7 in. (18 cm)

White-crowned Sparrow
Zonotrichia leucophrys
To 8 in. (20 cm)

Savannah Sparrow
Passerculus sandwichensis
To 6 in. (15 cm)
Note yellowish eyebrow.

Chipping Sparrow
Spizella passerina
To 5 in. (13 cm)
Note chestnut cap.

American Goldfinch
Spinus tristis
To 5 in. (13 cm)

Evening Grosbeak
Coccothraustes vespertinus
To 8 in. (20 cm)

Western Meadowlark
Sturnella neglecta
To 9 in. (23 cm)

Dark-eyed Junco
Junco hyemalis
Five related 'races' all have a dark hood and light outer tail feathers.

'Oregon' Race

'Slate-colored' Race